More Praise for *tender gr*

"Such intimate knowledge of place tethers the ecopoet ...eman's *tender gravity* to the land and seas around her home in A ...laska. There is sorrow in these poems—for a murdered brother who is remembered in the haunting lines of 'the warm dark,' and for all the oil spills, global warming, the vanishing species—but also serenity and a piercing love. The poems' longing for enlightenment is fulfilled not through renunciation but through closer and closer attention to the actual light 'that breathes wide // up mountainside to ridgeline across alpine field studded with lichen-red rocks,' the 'light / glinting off cobalt pool,' the 'light mediating fields awash in tasseled grass / to burn luminous amber.' This is a beautiful book."

—Ann Fisher-Wirth, author of *The Bones of Winter Birds*

"Marybeth Holleman's *tender gravity* is a thoroughly absorbing collection whose poems range from personal epiphanies to works with larger philosophical implications. They cover a wide range of emotions, including grief for a murdered brother and celebrations of the beauties and consolations of nature. Some of the poems are reminiscent of the work of the wonderful nature poet Mary Oliver, and at least one is Whitman-like in its expansiveness."

—John Morgan, author of *The Moving Out*

"The poems in *tender gravity* by Marybeth Holleman are truly gems, beautifully honed to cast and reflect the inner and outer light of her subjects. Many of her poems reveal and enhance details of the skies and seas, lands, mountains, flora, and fauna of our most northern State: 'Whales at Night,' 'The Fantastic Skies of the Orphan Stars,' 'How to Grieve a Glacier.' Her words and their cadences also offer new perspectives on experiences in our daily lives: 'Yesterday on a Familiar Trail,' 'The Remembered Earth,' and many more. Holleman's book is a remarkable treasure."

—Pattiann Rogers, author of *Quickening Fields*

"'What if / you could hold / forty times/ your weight / in love?' writes Marybeth Holleman in her poem 'Sphagnum,' which lingers, exploring the marvels of moss. As well as delighting in its attention to its subject, the poem also turns on its willingness to find in this rich green sponge some guidance for how to live a human life as well. *tender gravity* is full of moments like this, which fathom happiness among sundews and simultaneously mourn and delight in melting glaciers. Holleman looks carefully for her teachers in unexpected places: one poem speaks of a dead wolf left to brine in cold water for a season, then brought up so that we can admire the skull. Among Holleman's teachers—wolf skull, sundew, glacier, and moss—is also loss itself, her own process of fathoming the murder of her brother. As these poems move through a big Alaskan landscape and also bend in attention to grief, they seek and find temporary refuge 'in the variations in / the beat of a heart.' 'Every wisdom slips away / as soon as I try to name it,' Holleman says, but what slips also shimmers, caressed in Holleman's keen attentions. *tender gravity* is a book of hunger, and of restoration."

—Tess Taylor, author of *Rift Zone*

tender gravity

tender gravity

poems

Marybeth Holleman

Book design by Daniela Connor

Library of Congress Cataloging-in-Publication Data

Names: Holleman, Marybeth, author.
Title: Tender gravity: poems / Marybeth Holleman.
Description: First edition. | Pasadena: Boreal Books, an imprint of Red
  Hen Press, [2022]
Identifiers: LCCN 2022021248 (print) | ISBN 9781597099370 (paperback) |
  ISBN 9781597099523 (ebook)
Subjects: LCGFT: Poetry.
Classification: LCC PS3608.O4845665 T46 2022 (print) | LCC PS3608.O4845665
  (ebook) | DDC 811/.6—dc23
LC record available at https://lccn.loc.gov/2022021248
LC ebook record available at https://lccn.loc.gov/2022021249

The National Endowment for the Arts, the Los Angeles County Arts Commission, the
Ahmanson Foundation, the Dwight Stuart Youth Fund, the Max Factor Family Foundation,
the Pasadena Tournament of Roses Foundation, the Pasadena Arts & Culture Commission
and the City of Pasadena Cultural Affairs Division, the City of Los Angeles Department of
Cultural Affairs, the Audrey & Sydney Irmas Charitable Foundation, the Meta & George
Rosenberg Foundation, the Albert and Elaine Borchard Foundation, the Adams Family
Foundation, Amazon Literary Partnership, the Sam Francis Foundation, and the Mara W.
Breech Foundation partially support Red Hen Press.

First Edition
Published by Boreal Books
An imprint of Red Hen Press
www.borealbooks.org
www.redhen.org

Acknowledgments

Many thanks to the publications in which the following poems previously appeared:

8th World Wilderness Congress Poetry Award: "And the Geese Redeem Me"; *A Year of Being Here*: "Yesterday, on the familiar trail"; *Alaska Magazine*: "East Fork" (as part of "The Questions We Ask: A Quartet"); *Canary*: "another form," "Birch I," "Campbell Creek, August 5th," "Refugium," "Whales at Night," "Yesterday, on the familiar trail"; *Cirque*: "At a Poetry Reading," "every rock," "Rock Poem," "The Beating Heart, Minus Gravity," "The Fantastic Skies of Orphan Stars," "the warm dark," "Yesterday, on the familiar trail"; *Cold Mountain*: "Orionid"; *Cordella*: "skull"; *Deep Wild Journal*: "Not the Moon", "Whales at Night," "Yesterday, on the familiar trail"; *Entropy*: "Birch I," "Sphagnum," "Sundew: from that which appears inconsequential"; *Ice Floe: International Poetry of the Far North*: "Dispatch from Siberia," "Geminid," "Marbled Murrelets," "Prodigal" (as "Each Spring"); *ISLE: Interdisciplinary Studies in Literature and the Environment, Oxford UP*: "How to Grieve a Glacier," "Passing Through the Barren Islands," "The Outer Coast"; *Orion*: "Fortuitous"; *Poetics for the More-Than-Human World*: "with"; *Rewilding: Poems for the Environment*: "Dispatch from Siberia," "How to Grieve a Glacier"; *The Hopper*: "skating after many moons"; *Wards*: "Culross Passage, Five Months After"; and *Writing Nature*: "In the Garden, Early May."

Every book is a collaborative effort, and this one's no different. I'm grateful for all the humans who helped bring this book to life, especially Lisa Couturier (without whom), Peggy Shumaker, Carol Hult, Ellery Akers, Liz Bradfield, Ann Fisher-Wirth, Joeth Zucco, and, always, my son, James Holleman, and my husband, Rick Steiner.

CONTENTS

I

II

III

for the birch tree who watched over every word

tender gravity

I

The Beating Heart, Minus Gravity

when i was a young girl

i wondered what flying

would feel like

the kind where you stroke

through air like water

that's why i loved to swim

loved most of all

to dive deep

and then arc up

toward bubbles rising

to the bright light

but now and again

i dream of diving

to the blue depth

and rising, rising, following

bubble after bubble, seeing

golden sunlight glinting above

but never reaching

no matter how hard i kick

the tender gravity of air

Prodigal

Each spring
I learn
the songs of the returning ones
of fair voices filling
once-still air:

single-note bell
of the varied thrush
lilting crisp scale
of American robin
high-pitched waterfall
of ruby-crowned kinglet
ululations
of sandhill crane

making the blood in my veins
rush faster in the necessary cycle.

Woven through are tunes
of the familiars:
chickadee, nuthatch, redpoll, siskin.

Who would I rather be?
One returning,
or one staying?
I cup my ears
toward the breathy trill
of the dark-eyed junco.

To stay
and be taken for granted.
To return
and be regaled for it.

And you?
To have the upturned faces
searching only for you?

Or to be the one all winter
who reminds the sky
of its promise to wings.

Rock Poem

awed by the patterns, i say

      "   i'd like to be here with a geologist
and you say

      "   one was here once, an old guy who said,

           wow, this is some

ugly   rock. and i'm thinking

that is the last

      word i'd use to describe it.   "   ugly, he meant

tortured, he knew the processes that led to these

      starburst scrolling fractures

      white scribbles across gray

      orange shimmering splashes undercut

      by green

        he knew these colorpatterns

        evidenced a long

mutilation   of bedrock granite. but for me,

      sitting on the headland, it's the epitome

        of beauty, draws my gaze again and

again, the lines are messages scrawled by

giants

the Earth is   "   speaking to me in a language

I do not

yet

understand.

another form

shards of ice splitting
from the glacier's face
released from centuries
of hard labor. palpable
the relief, as sharp angles
shed to shining curves,
drips and puddles slip
into ocean, stream, lake.
purple clouds and the rain.
rounded rocks stippled
with lichens. alders and
willow wave. spruce crown
with eagle's nest blooming
blue forget-me-nots.
cormorant dive for herring,
humpback calf rolling
with a pod of leaping porpoise.
lion's mane jelly pulsing
over lemon-green popweed
and barnacled rock.
many hands grasping
big blue ferry's railing,
steady across spacious
seas toward the city
where they wing to distant
homes. grassy shores
and blooming roses. fields
of wheat and rising dough.
amber glow of cut glass
windows sifting winter's
snowsoft light.

The Fantastic Skies of Orphan Stars

I rejoice to live in such a splendidly disturbing time.
—Helen Keller

Perhaps I've been searching
too close to ground.
Perhaps I'm wrong to think
every answer lies beneath my feet.
Giving life should be enough to ask
of one blue sphere spinning in the dark.

Oh, to be an orphan star,
to see my birthplace from the outside,
the blue-white brilliance
encircled by yellow spirals,
the whole spinning parent galaxy,
and then to move slowly away
into the safety of the void.

East Fork

for Louise Murie, *1912-2012*

On the porch I think of her sitting here, husband perched on a ridge upriver, waiting for pups to emerge or adults to return to the den across the East Fork. Done with morning chores around the one-room cabin, she may have risen, walked down to the stream for water, and been stopped, as have I, by sweet scent of northern bedstraw, by rows of equisetum shimmering in morning light, by river beauties nodding fuchsia faces over clear-running waters. She may have wondered whether cinquefoil was related to rose, if gentian grew on other continents. So many blossoms at her feet; in one week I've seen fifty species. She collected, pressed roots, stems, leaves, flowers. Sent them to a friend in Maine, a lichen specialist in Norway, a botanist in Sweden. Louise among the first to classify the plants of Denali National Park, as Adolph was to study its sheep and wolves and bears, first to urge their protection. Pioneers, the Muries, like these river beauties I sit beside, watching the stream tug powdered leaves. In the Cathedral Range these flowers pour down either side of steep-falling waters, a long, billowing scarf. At Wonder Lake they fringe lakeside. Near Thoroughfare Pass they slip between rocks and willow. Fireweed their other common name as they're the first flowering plant to colonize after fire, first to succeed after ice: they cling to granite walls revealed by receding glaciers. I porch-sit in evening light and watch their agreeing heads. In a few weeks, pink petals will fall, pistils will swell, split, and send puffs of seed like starlight out into the air to settle where wind carries pioneers: someplace new, undiscovered, and lit from within.

Sphagnum

Imagine
being able
to pull
water
from deep
below
to the
surface
where you live.
Imagine
being able
to hold
forty times
your weight
of that which
you most
require.
What if
it were love?
What if
you could hold
forty times
your weight
in love?
And what
if in that
holding
you
expanded,
buoyant,
and strong,
more
your
self.

Want

It is our first full day together,
four of us, an uneasy alliance made
so hastily we don't know
if all the gear will fit into our kayaks.
Departing late, in rain, we paddle
toward Skiff Passage, narrow
opening to the outer coast. We want
to paddle the passage on outgoing
tides as if down a river.
We want to feel the winds of wilderness
in the cells of our bodies,
covered as they are with wet
raingear and the thin membrane
of our pale dry skins. We want
passage. Passage
into another kind of life, one not
encumbered by the little dramas
we create to believe our lives
are worth something more than
every single breath.

But we are late, and miss high
tide. At first it flows our way,
our thin boats needing only a sliver
of clear water over which to pass.
Then one, and another, grounds
out on gravel and barnacle, so
we line our boats along the edge,
soft rain stippling water like a
childhood game of jacks, simple
as the life of a barnacle (float until
you find a place to attach. lie on
your back. kick food into your
mouth. close at low tide.) I watch
their feathery legs dance
and try not to step on them,
my rubber boots clambering
heavy-footed intruder.

A widening, a deepening,
water enough to glide through,
a circle of quiet, Middle Bay.
Midpoint between Sitka spruce
forests carpeted in moss so soft
we could sleep away our lives,
and sharp rock headlands tufted with
windthrown grasses, the outer coast,
fronting the wide open Gulf of Alaska,
long reach to mainland interrupted
only by a clutch of islands so devoid
of trees they are called the Barrens
yet thrum with seabirds and whales
and thick forests of bull kelp. This
is what we paddle toward, out
of the middle and into a passage
to the sea. We want to reach
the outer coast. We want the vast
to cleanse transgressions we carry
whether done by or against us,
the heavy burden of them
enough to sink a ship.

Wet cold, we stop, huddle
under the last large spruce
and sip hot soup. On the far shore,
a deer, wide ears turned
toward us, paces tideline,
dropping her head to graze. Then,
having picked up the scent
of the unknown, she begins
to trot. Behind her, movement
as if her shadow kept its own pace:
a fawn, so small and dark that it
shapeshifts into a current of energy
and when still, is gone. The doe leaps
a straight upward pronk that sails her
over beach ryegrass and into forest,
and the tiny energy follows like dust
at her feet. We want them to stay,
we want them to be unafraid,
we want to leap like that,
we want to belong.

Paddling hard against incoming
tide we long last reach the outer
coast, wideness of blue meeting blue
where sea otters live among bull kelp
so thick that long fronds wrap
around the paddle, pulling us back
as if to say we have forgotten
something, there is more we have not
seen. But time and tides urge us
onward, and our wants, fickle, shift,
shadows lengthen even in midsummer
enough to pull us toward the cabin,
where we will go inside,
where we will light the lamps
and fire up the woodstove,
where we will shed, and shed
each wet layer down
to our still-pale skin and stand
in that uneasy warmth
even as every pore opens
wide as a mouth to ask that we
step outside once more.

At a Poetry Reading

I sit in the crowded auditorium
listening to the old man read
poems he wrote thirty years ago.
In his face lifted
      to the light
his eyes like large pools
      of memory
shine a kind of fire
I have not seen
in a very long time.

When I am eighty years old,
will I be able to stand
      with such power
arcing like lightning bolts
      around my body?
Will I contain words that have meaning
beyond their first spoken breath?

As I, along with hundreds of others,
sigh at the poem's last line,
his eyes hold the light a moment longer
and that's when I see:

we could be a stand of pine trees in shadow,
blades of sedge on a dewy meadow,
hatch of mayflies over a slow-moving stream,
and he would still
      stand that way
      speak that way
his eyes would still
      blaze that way.

Geminid

—Hanalei, Kauai

they say you will rain down tonight
just above Orion's reach
the geometry of Gemini open to hold
fallen sky light
so I walk to a dip in the road
where tropical forest hides house lights
and golf course opens sky
head up-tilted, eyes shielded
from carfuls of teenagers calling
to each other in the dark, singing
the long arc of their light-years lives
cruising with the everlasting
stars and brief spirals of meteors
flash
one burns out just below Gemini
momentary strand of dying light
followed by a clack not from above
but from something here on earth
living in dark as in light
the albatross I saw in daylight
three I took for teenagers
play-acting courtship
having alighted on land
after three years of open seas
now they clack hard beaks
follow their albatross hearts in the dark
flash
thin light streak on the edge of vision
o how this night brims with light.

Marbled Murrelets

at first light
they lift from beds of moss
high in the arms of spruce
thread dawn flyways at 100 mph
weave forest and river and ridge
tiny brown projectiles
burst into blue expanse
dive beneath waves
zip together two familiars:
tree and sea:
all of it home.

In the Garden, Early May

I mean to sit and write
but outside my window the birch
that drapes the drive
unfurls bright green, and
trollius and geraniums push
pale heads from soil still
damp from snowmelt, and
spruce, so dark and brooding
all winter, light tiny fires at every
tousled tip, and
I can't stand to simply watch.

Who is to say how a day's
best spent? At the end
of a life, what remains?
A few scattered pages—
some of them read—
maybe one bright phrase
that clings to the world immortal—
like the seeds of birch
so many and small, yet
each may grow into a tree
taller than a library, and as useful.

My life is lived like this, choosing
whether to record or experience—
knowing one without the other
lacks meaning, and yet wondering

whether meaning is overrated—
believing Thomas Berry right to say
The purpose of life is existence,
and self-delight in existence.

I apologize to the god of words
but the god of dirt calls to me
calls to me
now.

Birch I

Branches reach and then break
    in winds and snows,
then rebuild and rebreak,
    again and again:
transforming suffering to beauty,
    one leaf at a time.

The Outer Coast

I have dreamed
this have dreamed
long swells rocking
light swaying westward,
round blue sea meeting
only lambent sky,
fine eelgrass ribboning
green to otherwise blue.
from where this
longing for something
beyond familiar? for
floating far from
ground, where surface
yields to cresting humpback
and spangles with puffin
wingbeats? remote
as stars glinting among
undulations of kelp
this outer coast and yet
home to some
primigenial memory
of when I, like these
moon jellies slipping
by, spent days aimlessly
aimed for what
I could not yet see.

II

Sundew: from that which appears inconsequential

here you are:

tiny rosette of red

hugging this wet mound

of ground. here: where

I have learned

to find you: down

low where the winged

might land, wanting

your sweet nec-

tar to sip but stick

they do, stuck,

and your ten-

tacles hold tight,

so small and dewy

like morning's

first soft and

harmless light.

How to Grieve a Glacier

It's not something you can hold in your arms.
You can't rock with its image in a blanket
and keen away the nearing pain.

That white face is distant, and cold, unrelenting
in its forward grind to the sea,
stalwart even as it thins, crumbles, pulls back
into history and oblivion.

The sun itself finds nothing to love,
save soft rivulets of water its rays release
from eons of hard frozen luck.

But I tell you I do love this blue-white giant,
and grieve its leaving, even as I thrill to watch
thunderbolts of ice crash into azure seas.

So we sit, you and I, scanning the newly revealed
and imagining what next will show itself,
what balded rock and bared shoreline,
as ice slips and pulls away in great chunks.

We know it is leaving, abandoning us
to what our kind has created,
and we know its gift of rarified water
will only bring more sorrow.

Yet it is a gorgeous deterioration.
Glowing face of one turned toward
what the living cannot see.

Bright Sungrazing Comet II

Today dawns dark again,
January drafting under the door
and stippling water
along the windowsill.
Inside it's warm and light
where I've lit candles
that echo what's to come,
but dark is what I yearned for
last time back south to family
when the sun's glare lit
a frenzy I could not enter,
when I wanted only dark's truth
that everything under the sun
comes and goes with no concern
for our confusing dramas,
just as the comet grazing
so close to the surface
of our necessary sun
is, as I sit in blessed dark,
plunging to its timely death.

Skull

It's been in our family
for nearly twenty years,
killed across the calm
waters of the sound
on verdant spring flats
of the wide-mouthed delta.
The skinned body left
in a dumpster, he, part
scientist, part lover, dived
the dump to retrieve,
to sink it into saltwater
below his office on the docks.
Fishing boats swayed, left,
returned, filled with fish,
with snow, ice, meltwater,
swayed, left. He pulled up
from sea the young wolf's
skeleton, and parceled
out sea-scoured bones
to friends and their children,
some who grew to be
trappers wanting more
than bone. Some carried
their bone like talisman. Some
trying to gain strength
in the wake of a cancer
ground theirs and drank.
One gripped the bone so tight
in death that fingers
had to be pried open. The skull
he kept, gave, when we joined,
to me, sits on my top shelf,
brought down while I wrote
of a man who gave his life

to studying wolves, wanting
us to see how they, too,
care for their young and each
other, wanting us
to see past tooth and claw
to tender underbelly.

This skull smooth
with time and the sea, I lift
it to the shelf, book done,
bottled message out,
and feel in my finger
a sharp pain. Quick bite.
A splinter, bone shard, under
my skin and I don't pull it out.

Culross Passage, Five Months After

—*Prince William Sound, August 1989*

        from the beach

we see

        something swimming straight
        to us from Culross Island to mainland.
           too clumsy for

sea

        otter, but what else could it

be, sea

        otter addled ~~by oil~~
        is all we can

imagine.

        five months after ~~the spill~~,
           ~~cleanup~~ operations ceased,
        we can't

find

        a beach not splattered
           by ~~tar~~ balls, absorbent pads, ~~oil~~.
        closer, we

see white

        fur, white back hump, two small
           black horns, narrow face:
        mountain goat
           clambers onto a low headland
        near us and stands, quivering,

facing us, legs

        wobbling, half-frozen,
        stamps each foot,
        shakes her head,
        stamp and shake for over an hour,
        then slips,

disappears into

        thick spruce forest. and I'm ~~told~~
           by wildlife biologists that

mountain goats ~~don't~~ come to saltwater,
~~don't~~ swim, ~~don't~~ live on Culross Island,
they know ~~what~~ they know,
I know what

I saw.

thoughts on a black bear, charging

she does not wish us harm.
i do not wish her harm.
i wish to pass, unharmed, along the trail.
she wishes to pass, her cubs unharmed, through the woods.
but here we are,
walking a familiar trail in a soft rain, my two dogs in front.
then a skritch skritch skritch and the dog in front barks.
two cubs up two spruces, one dog with me and the other,
the barking one, separated from me by her,
black fur rippling like waves of grass as she turns
to my dog, then to me, back and forth.
my dog barks, and she turns, four quick gallops,
and my dog dashes away.
she turns to my other dog, now leashed, and me,
now holding a can of bear spray and yelling words
i no longer remember.
she does not wish us harm.
we do not wish her harm.
we only wish to pass unharmed.
she only wishes to pass, her cubs unharmed.
the light rain falls.
in this weather she was not expecting us.
i will not find her here on sunny days,
when bikes and horses and walkers stream by.
but today, light rain, and a bear, protecting her cubs.
her black face, brown eyes and snout, framed by perfect darkness.
a beauty, even in distress. she shakes that luscious fur. then
gallops towards us, me talking loudly, her stopping
as we back up, back and back. she swings around,
my other dog returns, barking, wanting to get to me.
no, i am sure i say no, and i keep backing up, and she charges
my dog again, who again flees, and i back, back down the trail,
the hill, to go around below her, to hope to find my dog
somewhere ahead, safe, and in one piece.

she does not wish us harm.
we do not wish her harm.
only passage, only passage.
she is above us on the hill, somewhere, hidden by forest,
and could, if she wanted to harm us,
sprint down and be on us within seconds.
but it would take her away, farther, from her tree-clinging cubs.
i walk, and talk, make noise, watch upslope, while above
all is quiet. around her far around we go,
and there is my dog, running towards me, quickly
submitting to the leash, all of us knowing
how close we came.

Farther

This, engraved on a bench in the Alaska Botanical Gardens: "One is nearer God's heart in a garden than anywhere else on Earth." I'm no longer religious but these words feel true. Hands in soil, I steady, closer to root, more able to handle what life heaves my way. Had I lost my brother in June, I'd have gone to the garden and pulled weeds when anger rose, anger at his killer, anger at absent gun laws, anger at the meth that addled the killer's brain, anger that my gorgeous little brother would never grow old, never be a grandfather, never speak my name again. I could've gone to the garden, dug and pulled, yanked out the rampant nettles and then, calmed from exertion, fallen to my knees and planted fragrant white roses. But he was shot in January. It was dark. All was frozen. My garden waited under four feet of snow, a faint but steady pulse. I hung a punching bag in the garage. Bought bright pink boxing gloves to hide the bloody knuckles.

Out

The tops of the spruce seem to move
though there isn't a breath of wind
and they don't sway as one but instead
each needle, it shimmers as if—

In central America, people are using
nothing but sight to record
the respiring breath of each plant
from leaf to rainforest air:

to see a plant exhale.

My teacher says all violence
would subside, if not disappear
if each of us, everywhere, just
paid attention to our breath.

in. then out.

It's so easy we don't even have
to think about breathing but when
I listen and wait for call and response,
I learn there's just so much I—

A scientist claims that the breath
of plants can save us from
warming climates and acid seas
if only we'd re-green our world.

to relax, exhale twice as long.

Once I sat on a rock that had
recently been under a river of ice,
shaped now by the softest green moss
so gently it felt like a breath.

Refugium

after A.R. Ammons' *"Love Song"*

At dusk, when the light
falls away from your slopes
and the line of your rippled ridge
sharpens against the golden
afterglow from the setting sun,
you with your halo don't go,
watch over me as I lay upon
your soft treed arms and let
the cooling breeze of night
descend upon me, spent.
I climbed so long to get here,
to reach the ridgeline of your lips,
to fall to my knees in wonder
at all that lies at your feet, vast
in all directions. More than I can
hold in my arms, say with my
tongue, more, I want to stay
on your sturdy shoulders and wait
out the storm sure to come, the one
we have set upon ourselves with
our desire to have, to have, to have.
Let me remain here with you, large
and immoveable rock, mountain,
let you be my whole world.

Bishop Rock

should clouds appear to wash the sky with shadows,

recall what hides behind. there is more to a tale

than what the teller reveals. what is hidden,

left unsaid, holds the greater weight.

see this feather lying here, once on a black-white bird.

i watched it fall and settle, i watched it float back up.

the deer that stood on water, the rocks beneath my feet,

all rose as one and carried off the missing and forgotten.

head held back, yet i could not envision where they'd go.

white-capped the mountains, falling still, a howling

in the wind. voices raised, they follow in that ocean

made of dust. it won't be long until we all know.

December 21, 2016

The volcanic eruption of 1912 in Katmai was the largest of the twentieth century.

In these months of dark coming from all sides,
an election gone haywire with four years of insanity rising,
as we dance our crazy, crazy, really, everything coming from *homo sapiens*,

nothing we're doing or have done or want makes any sense,
I am reeling with wanting some sense,

so I pass on a solstice skate party, on a holiday literary party,
and go alone to a geology lecture.
The scientist begins with history and I am restless:

I do not want to hear human dramas interpret the landscape.
I want rock-hard truth: the kind ancient stone holds:

I want to revel in the ground that carries a story infinitely older than us.
Older than greed, anger, hate. Older than insanity.
Finally the story moves beyond us, through botanists at the volcanic eruption.

And I don't care about their journey's travails, slim rations, blistered feet.
I care about the plants they found, or didn't.

The fumaroles. The ignimbrite flow. Pyroclastic material.
Airfall: the material that arrived by air, burst skyward from the eruption.
Measure the depth of airfall. Measure the depth of ignimbrite.

Determine the source of eruption. Not the mountain with three peaks gone.
It is that mound, on the Mars plain. Novarupta. New.

The eruption shrouded Alaska, British Columbia.
Its acid ate away bedsheets hanging to dry in Seattle.
The ash dropped global temperatures one degree for a full year.

A power, a force so great and out of human control.
I settle in my seat.

The Summer Garden

—Saint Petersburg

It's easy to imagine,
within the embrace of these dark trunks
and alabaster statues,
the swish of billowing dresses
and gentle voice of the empress
addressing her attendants.

It's easy to imagine that any
compassion Catherine ever had
toward her legions of subjects enduring
outside these gardens, in the slant
light of Peter's great city,
arose here, within these cool greens,
from birdsong, or the scent of a white
bloom, or the praise of leaves
in the summer breeze.

When history books are written,
what do they say of the influence of
skies, and trees? That the sun shone,
that the fury of hailstorms rained upon
royal crowns, that linden fell like dominoes
when heads rolled in the streets,
that the great siege of 1941 was overcome
because the weary could lie here,
beneath this soft green canopy,
and sigh out their hunger into the gentle air,
see it winged to promise.

And the Geese

They waft in, from up and down the greenbelt
which is nothing more than
a small stream running through a big city,
water far from clear,
brambled banks contained by an asphalt bike path,
graveled playgrounds, baseball fields, parking lots.

Yet all this week,
at the dark end of dusk,
I've walked to where the stream widens into a lagoon,
just to watch them arrive:
waves of Canada geese,
from the manicured lawns of
the oil company complex,
the city golf course,
and thousands upon thousands of yards,

to settle here, on this quiet lens,
appearing with a crescendo of trumpeting calls,
big wings and wide webbed feet angled for the landing,
hovering
over power lines and buildings and down, down onto this circle,
alighting
effortlessly onto this small space amidst an ocean of concrete,
gliding
feather to feather, a thousand or more, on the transformed water,
one act of redemption every evening,
until ice edges the lagoon and they wing south.

Orionid

—Mount Lemmon, Arizona, 1986

Sparks from Halley's Comet
in the black hole of a predawn sky
revive the chars of memory
when I was happy atop a mountain
in the desert, when you and I
were young and together
believed the world lay before us.
The caretaker with more wine
than he alone could drink
ushered us into the globe rooms
that perched on the mountain
like tethered moons,
showed us that streaming light
from far away so close
my fingers tingled with imagined
touch. We knew then
the importance of light, knew
this was our one lifetime's chance,
as we followed faint yellow strips
back down switchbacks
through spruce to saguaro,
from snow to sand,
we knew what mattered.
But what we didn't know,
even as we watched
the comet's ephemeral light,
tail always chasing after,
was how to hold on.

the faint white curve of the moon

the faint white curve of the moon
lights apparitions outside my window
sends a chill across my bare arms
to my fingers, motionless
on the keyboard.

what is there to say
that would matter
to the moon, and the dead bears?
can language return what is lost—
the brother, the bears, belief
in this world?

when my brother was murdered,
suddenly i did not fear death,
thought i'd been forced
to ease my chokehold on life.
but it was a temporary grace,
flashover that numbed pain,
jolt born of life's own grip,

so the death of eleven white bears
sears through me like a white hot sword
now that I know the pattern of grief
the endless
pattern of grief.

do not think, mother,
that i love a bear more than my brother.
think instead that i cannot distinguish
the variations in
the beat of a heart.

for all I know—
and what do I know?

every wisdom slips away
as soon as I try to name it.

Passing Through the Barren Islands

Fogbank reveals little surface
off the port side, our wake churning sea.
Pattern of skipping stone just beyond
scribes a murre paddling away,
too full or unconcerned
to fly, to dive. Brume lifts, veil thrown back,
revealing murre's home seas, passage
between the Barrens, mountains
rising from the Gulf of Alaska bare
save wildflowers, seabirds, the spray
of feeding humpbacks. In any direction
countless whale spouts mist air
as murres, puffins, scoters
dive and flap and paddle
away. I have been away
for weeks, and now turn homeward,
yearning to find all as it was.
Days out yet but the turn lightens me
as do these birds and whales in their
summer waters, blue as it should be. Yet
I recall murres, returned in spring
to oil, flailing away from our nets
but unable to fly—
white breasts stained black,
wings beating but not lifting.
They did not want rescue, could not find
refuge in dark boxes, crated
swimming ponds, sterile washing rooms.
What in their species memory
of these birth waters
shifted after that dark plague?
Will these murre fledglings,
who don't yet know that days here grow
shorter and colder, feel any pangs

at leaving, any delight next spring
at returning? Or is home wherever
their flock is, wherever they are,
dense shadow memories
blessedly lifted clear?

every rock

every rock remembers
the day I was born. remembers
the afternoon you learned
to walk. not even the slightest
wingbeat of a moth as sunlight lifts
early morning dew escapes their
notice. they witness and regard all
life with the tenderness of
a grandparent gazing on the new:
eyes that see far beyond anything
words could convey and yet
yearn, regardless, for the happiness
of the child. I know this is so.
but I don't know what rocks make of it.
my life, yours, they seem content
with how we've turned out
but when asked if we're doing
what we were put here for, they are
silent. I press both palms hard against
their solid coolness, and all they say is,
do not think too much of your life.
then like an echo off granite cliffs
once covered in ice I hear,
do not think too much of all life.
it is a sweet interlude in the turbulence.
we will be missed.

III

Yesterday, on the familiar trail

A routine walk, you know the kind: your mind
is far away, and it's just your bones walking,
marking the rhythm of heartbeat to footstep.
It's always like this right before you see them,

the ones who never take an absentminded step,
staring at you with heads lowered, ears erect,
paws spread wide and hackles half-raised,
golden eyes deciding whether you're predator
or prey. What other category do they need?
What other thought? It's you,

with your thousand and one concepts, who must
step back toward that joy-sap rising, step back
into the only world that is.

Dispatch from Siberia

They live and work along the northern edge of land
where ice touches down every fall, later and later now,
and not as far south, so that walrus—tens of thousands
of long-toothed soft brown bodies—have immigrated
farther north and now gather just outside
their towns, beach en masse and wait for the ice
which is later and later, so that these men,
with their wide stances and wider smiles, armed with nothing
but sticks and the sense that generations of northern living
have given them, pray to their spirits and protect those walrus,
at first from polar bears, moving in waves along the coast,
roaming wide in search of food, following scent of walrus
and then carried out on that ice, staying with ice as it
recedes so far that they have not come back, those bears,
to this shore, and are either drowned or starved or moved
to other shores, Canada or Greenland, where ice still stays near,
and now from curious townspeople and foreign tourists,
circling near and clicking cameras and causing stampedes
in which thousands, pups and their mothers, are trampled
to death, so these brave men, armed with nothing
but sticks and a belief in the world they inhabit, carry
the carcasses far from town, leave them to feed
passing polar bears, and the first year, over one hundred bears
came and ate every morsel, but since then, with the ice
carrying the bears away, the mound of carcasses remains
rotting on the tundra, on this northern shore
where these men, smiles as wide as ever, continue to believe.

All the Notes

Birds can hear both relative and absolute pitch, more temporal fine structure
(similar to timbre) than humans, and all of it faster than us—
so they hear more notes than we do.

I am glad I cannot hear all the notes they sing.

It is already more than I can keep in my muddied head.

This one, then that one, each of them singing feathered bodies out the treetops.

Songs spiral down to me like maple seeds, slight helicopters of sound.

They are a web that nets my senses.

They are Indra's net, each of them shining something never before seen.

And from this half-heard orchestra, they find each other.

And from this tumbled forest, they heave a hidden nest.

From snatches of twigs and moss and insects smaller than my iris, raise a family.

And just before summer's true onset, they fledge and fly.

Their lives more brief than a half-held breath, and filled with a half-heard

    melody.

In these treetops, the feathers of my days floating up.

The lotus in the pond knows the score.

The lotus in the pond hears every single note.

the warm dark

we walk the blackened road
while sounds in the jungle call to us
    in their strange night language
        (clack and croak
        clatter and
        murmur and sing
sounds we don't know, and it's the
not-knowing that soothes.
we meander, only stars
lighting our way, white-yellow glimmer of
    orion and the milky way
vast wheel of countless stars so near our own.
i feel closest to you here, this warm dark
familiar in our childhood but now
    where i live so far north
as unknown as these sounds in the night.
        (when it's warm, there's no dark
        when dark, no warmth.
my skirt swings soft against
    bare legs, wavering quiet—
with sight shut low the other senses rise.
i miss this, standing idly gazing up
    only barely hoping for a shooting star.
i can't tell anyone, not the least our grieving mother,
that i feel closer to you now than when you were alive.
that in death, my brother, you walk with me,
    the breeze your hand
and we are ten and eight, gathering neighbors
for a game of kick the can—the scuffling feet,
scurrying to hide, the count, the call, the search.
never
    was i afraid when you were
    somewhere in that dark.
never

did i give up my hiding spot.
it was you gave me courage to make that dash for the can,
you when our mother refused to see me.
     (night walks the times
      i felt safe near her.
by your life,
   your own bright dash to it—
little brother my star.

Not the Moon

We hike up to Blueberry Hill while the sky behind us glows to orange, long sunset of January gilding our city. Dry snow squeaks under boots until we stop, hear what makes our dog stand still as stone: ravens winging to roost, carving cold air into lullaby. *Hush, hush, hush,* they sing, dark sickles overhead. Orange deepens to red and melts skyline behind us as we round the corner to face jagged peaks from which we think the moon will rise. We sit on snow with backs to rock. Blue sky, purple sky, deep sky. Blue snow, purple snow, deep snow. Ravens call from we know not where, then a third strokes sky overhead and is joined by the two calling, all three heading upvalley single file. Last light glances a curve of white mountain against powder-blue dusk when my husband says, *There.* Over a smooth lip in craggy ridge, sliver of silver grows quick as sunrise at the equator and not moonrise near the pole. I sit stock still, snow cold seeping, and try to feel how it is not the moon lifting up into view but us, this Earth, that is slowly spinning. For a moment, for a halfmoment, I do sense that I am turning, enough to grow dizzy and touch fear, brief as cloud wisp, of falling off, away, into stars. It's too much, the rolling of our home orb, only invisible gravity holding us, so we call this moon*rise*, give moon all credit for this brilliance slipping up, over the ridge, oval stretching to circle of light. We say the moon is full though it is always full. We say the sun sinks, and slides, scraping the horizon red. We say ravens winging to roost do not have thought or language like ours, so though it appeared that two called the third, we second-guess it, spinning ourselves again. We say whatever works to keep the ground beneath our feet solid, this boulder pressing my shoulder blades unmoving, even as we twirl like snowflakes, like motes of moonshine, giddy in the light.

Campbell Creek, August 5th

they are there when you stop
and watch clear water's choreography
across multitude of patterned rock.
rippling length of crimson flashes
in pulsating current, thick as logs
but supple and swaying, the darker
tails waving side to side just enough
to stay in place. red swaths reveal
and disappear, one then another
then a line of five or more strung
like rubies light and dark shadow lilt
with one quick flick red rippling dissipates
then reappears against the shore
or limber in lines along a fallen tree. big
red muscles beating back up what as
fingerlings they each swept down now
the laboring push, the urgent
flame daubed dark swaying curves
tinged now late summer white tips
reminding mountains what will come.
five years of deep sea to return,
arrow-straight swim hundreds of ocean miles,
to this shallow stream fins slicing surface
frosted with their termination dust,
tails singing strong upcurrent as streaming
bodies pull them, fits and starts,
downriver, back to the orchestral sea.

Fortuitous

Stop telling me it's nothing, this

that has fallen from a tree, a shedding

of old skin. Just stop the worn

saw of your life's own emptiness.

Each morning you wake and breathe,

what a miracle, your lungs and heart working

all night long. The blood pulses in your veins,

the leaf unfurls and patters summer's shining

tune, then falls in a kind of graceful undoing you see

as an end, foreboding settling in like the darkest

woods. But I ask you to stop excavating for some

meaning beyond this piece of birch bark,

with the staccato of babyskin sounding dark mouths,

tender hands of lichen holding it in standing ovation,

a thin green spire housing the red mouth of the inchworm,

who emerges only when you fall still, and silent.

All of it, I tell you, every single hand and mouth,

wants to speak to you, yes to you, right now,

in the language of the world.

Whales at Night

they come
after the day's
fishing fleet
has gone to anchor
awaken us
with a sigh
that sounds human
but is whale-breath
the long exhale
after a deep dive
sprays dappling
concentric rings
left by their arcs
into air
on an otherwise
silent and glassy
sea

skating after many moons

it's a small lake, a pond, really, or not even that,
a wet meadow in summer where our one kind
of frog who contains some kind of antifreeze
in its veins lives, the only one can survive this far
north, our only amphibian, only cold-blooded being,
and when he was young, my boy, and I wanted
to keep him awake to the world, we came here
and listened to the frog chorus, recorded it for
a scientist cataloguing the city's frogs, who wanted
to see how changing weather was changing them,
would there be more or less, would they die out
as summers dried. she gave us a recording so we'd
know what to listen for, but there was no mistaking
the tender high notes, held and overlapping
like the rounds I sang at summer camp, calls unlike
the looping lilt of birds. now when I stand on this
frozen meadow, in white figure skates I got when
I was just a girl still in easy love with this world,
I hear all that's held under ice, since we recorded
the frog chorus, my boy grown to a man who
may or may not notice the frogs are leaving,
when I stand here seeking the certainty a child
feels about the world that holds her steady,
a mother feels for her boy holding her hand
as they cross the damp meadow and stand still,
listening, when I move, clumsily, cautiously,
afraid of reeling headfirst onto what might crack,
my limbs begin to remember, from my girlhood,
the few times the lake froze, and my dad took
all us kids there, swung us around, and
that one time I skated with a friend who flew
circles and arcs around my leaden feet, my limbs
fling it all and swing me around and around
until I am dizzy in love again, until the world
is aright and all this keeps me twirling.

The Remembered Earth

Once in his life a man ought to concentrate
his mind upon the remembered earth.
—N. Scott Momaday

I have never been here. This
whiteness, each small island
with its own dense ice shield
run to shore, such austere
terrain is new to me. I have never
witnessed commotion at thin slice
where land finds sea, each revealed
rock inhabited, wing and flipper,
scarce ribbon of sand reverbs
with steady pad of penguin feet.
I have never stood where white
is not just white, but color wheel
spinning all, green to gold, blue
to rose, ashimmer, where my own
heart feels larger as if I have never
before breathed such complete
air, have never filled my lungs.
Remember what I have not
seen. Remember from where
I must have come, where all life
once rose. And in that ray
of recognition, this: never
have I been gone from here.

Williwaw

it is about the light.
an expanse that breathes wide

up mountainside to ridgeline across alpine
field studded with lichen-red rocks
down scree slope long slip glide along
deep lake & black lake still snow-rimmed

to straight drop of raven granite
fanning to wash of rock & supine berries
to cerulean chain of slope-encircled lakes.

it is the light
glinting off cobalt pool
bouncing from rock spire to
sheep grazing far emerald hillside

illuminating the tips of horns
on one niveous atop cliff streaming
cloud-plummet waterfall.

penetrating multi-hued mountainside
rivulets of bright newgreen
meld to deepened green & blend
to golden to crimson.

embracing silver strand stream
descending downvalley
& purple sap-tipped hemlock cones

scribing season's transmutation
with each pearled drop.

light

mediating fields awash in tasseled grass
to burn luminous amber, a fire
that must be what Moses saw:

the burning bush, burnished light,
the light, the light, the light.

with

with steller jay tap tapping at the window for peanuts, telling me weather's cooling,
    winter comes.

with the line climbing the snowy mountainside, six in a row, black wolves.

with gazelle chased by cheetah, both so fleet, me saying no while my son says go.

with thin black cat laying two small fish on our doorstep for her kittens inside.

with my nephew's snake my young son holds in both hands.

with small black beetle whispering into the rock around my pansies.

with grosbeak's song tumbling light as dry snow down through the trees, asking for
    sunflower seeds.

with ground squirrel kits whose chatter reverberates through derelict gold mine
    pipe they make home.

with pulsating orbs of white spread below my kayak, a gathering of moon jellies,
    mirroring sky's clouds.

with three black snakes sunning together on a boulder in springtime woods.

with the spray of their exhale misting my face as two humpbacks leap from glowing
    seas.

with a dangling thread just before my eyes, inchworm hanging from the willow,
    green U-turning.

with adopted sun conure, whose shrieks still rainbow my ear though I regret not
    a moment of him on my shoulder, nibbling strands of my hair.

with small black puppy at Om beach, gnawing on a dead crab, the sacred bloated
    cow nuzzling a pile of trash nearby.

with black dog at my feet, soft groan as I stroke the silk of her back.

with river otters tumbling over one another along the barnacled shoreline, one head
    lifting when my shutter clicks.

with night bunny under the roses, beautiful bones ticking time's soft rhythm.

with black bear searching in hungry spring for birdseed we miss, batting at the
    garden hose, down on forearms to lap from the dogs' water bowl.

with the baby gang, chickadee nuthatch junco newly fledged, alighting in birch,
    learning the bird bath.

with bats, circling, at dusk, my head, dancing to my runner's high.

with gray squirrel high in the oak, scrambling to avoid the beebee shots of neighbor
    boys my mother chases, screaming, from our backyard.

with my husky racing over tundra like blossoming wind, quick becoming small as a
    seed.
with pair of mountain goats pressed against cliffs lining Crow Pass, watching hikers
    toil.
with two frogs under the lilacs, one who lived two decades, our own tuck
    everlasting.
with red fox trotting by our tent in the Arctic summer night, red tongue out,
    panting, so light-footed she leaves no prints in soft mud.
with bumblebee bouncing off the window, wanting the colors of flowers my walls
    wear.
with polar bear pushing black snout against the window I raise just in time, leaving
    in dusty glass a single paw print, shimmer by the night's aurora.
with king salmon in the stream, termination dust on their dorsals slowing tails to
    list into gentler current.
with the rolling thunder of hooves across my dreams,
    the licks of a thousand rough tongues,
    the harmony of songs lifted to limitless blue,
    every day and night, world without end.

Paper Clay

here, in the center
of what was once impenetrable,

I stand, both feet below
what is otherwise ground,

head in the atmosphere
of rock solid calm. I know

this is not possible, know
that the act of going

through not over
is not supposed to feel

this fine. where is that
sorrow who trailed me

like the last note of a dirge?
where the shouldered weight

that never would lighten?
here, deep among boulders

whose shadows tumble
at my feet, cascading space

weighted by invisible cloudsong
and the faint hope of lift,

I know, finally, without doubt,
what it is to be inside a mountain

and all I feel is a soaring joy.

Paper clay is the process of adding fiber to clay to create lighter structures. This poem was inspired by Annette Bellamy's art installation of suspended paper clay boulders.

52

Belonging is unquestionable. Just notice
how bones small as bird's wings hold you up.
Think back to grade school lessons
on the Roman arch, the keystone resting
between two spans, each stone carrying exactly
enough pressure to stay in place
without cracking or straining.

                                  Belonging
is unquestionable. Place your attention
upon what you can rely, each morning they fall
to the ground and do their work.
And you know, even if shoved
into tight darkness,
they will ground you as they lift you,
they will carry you like a feather
into and out of all your days, filled
as days are with mountains, light, and rain.

Why, just today
you watch a flock of redpolls fading
away and then appearing, hundreds of winged
missives waving their way down, fluttering
around each other like a mind
making itself up. You stand on your 52
bones and lean back, your body
weaving the sign of infinity into
the welcoming air.

Biographical Note

Marybeth Holleman is author of *The Heart of the Sound*, coauthor of *Among Wolves*, and coeditor of *Crosscurrents North*, among others. Pushcart Prize nominee and Siskiyou Prize finalist, she's published in venues including *Orion*, *The Guardian*, *Christian Science Monitor*, *Sierra*, *ISLE*, *AQR*, and *North American Review*. She taught women's studies and creative writing at University of Alaska and held artist residencies at Mesa Refuge, Hedgebrook, Tracy Arm-Fords Terror Wilderness, and Denali National Park. Raised in North Carolina's Smokies, she transplanted to Alaska's Chugach Mountains after falling head over heels for Prince William Sound two years before the oil spill. She lives in Anchorage, Alaska.

For more, visit www.marybethholleman.com.